The
HOMESCHOOL
Teacher's
Planner & Organizer

FOR THE ORGANIZED HOMESCHOOL TEACHER

STUDENT NAME

AGE

SCHOOL YEAR LEVEL

YEAR

The
HOMESCHOOL
Teacher's
Planner

SECTIONS

1. 12 Month Goals

2. Lesson Timetable

3. Attendance Log

4. Website & Resources Log

5. Important Dates

6. Weekly Lesson Planners

7. Major Assignment Log

8. Report Cards

notes.

12 Month Goals

Write down the goals you wish to achieve over the next 12 months

PERSONAL GOALS

....

....

....

....

HEALTH & FITNESS GOALS

....

....

....

....

HOMESCHOOL GOALS

....

....

....

....

WEEKLY TIMETABLE

DATE COMMENCING: /   /

DAY	MONDAY	TUESDAY	WEDNESDAY
LESSON 1 *START TIME* :	Subject	Subject	Subject
LESSON 2 *START TIME* :			
LESSON 3 *START TIME* :			
LESSON 4 *START TIME* :			
LESSON 5 *START TIME* :			

Other information to note

THURSDAY	FRIDAY	NOTES
Subject	Subject	

WEEKEND

YOUR HOMESCHOOL

Lesson Timetable

Print and stick your timetable below

USE THIS BLANK SPACE OR THE TEMPLATE TIMETABLE PROVIDED

Lesson Timetable

Print and stick your timetable below

USE THIS BLANK SPACE OR THE TEMPLATE TIMETABLE PROVIDED

ATTENDANCE LOG

MONTH

DAYS											
1											
2											
3											
4											
5											
6											
7											
8											
9											
10											
11											
12											
13											
14											
15											
16											
17											
18											
19											
20											
21											
22											
23											
24											
25											
26											
27											
28											
29											
30											
31											
TOTAL											

TOTAL DAYS PRESENT =

TOTAL DAYS ABSENT =

IMPORTANT WEBSITE RESOURCES

Name	Website Address

Other Books or Resources

IMPORTANT DATES

Record the import Homeschool Year Dates

MONTH:

MONTH:

MONTH:

IMPORTANT DATES

Record the import Homeschool Year Dates

MONTH:

MONTH:

MONTH:

IMPORTANT DATES

Record the import Homeschool Year Dates

MONTH:

MONTH:

MONTH:

IMPORTANT DATES

Record the import Homeschool Year Dates

MONTH:

MONTH:

MONTH:

Progress Tracker

What are my current Top 5 Priorities I need to action?

1. _____

_____ Target Date to Complete / /

2. _____

_____ Target Date to Complete / /

3. _____

_____ Target Date to Complete / /

4. _____

_____ Target Date to Complete / /

5. _____

_____ Target Date to Complete / /

Other Notes or Details

DATE / /

LESSON 1
SUBJECT
_____

Lesson Information/Assignment Task

Completed

LESSON 2
SUBJECT
_____

Lesson Information/Assignment Task

Completed

LESSON 3
SUBJECT
_____

Lesson Information/Assignment Task

Completed

LESSON 4
SUBJECT
_____

Lesson Information/Assignment Task

Completed

LESSON 5
SUBJECT
_____

Lesson Information/Assignment Task

Completed

DATE / /

LESSON 1
SUBJECT
_____

Lesson Information/Assignment Task

Completed

LESSON 2
SUBJECT
_____

Lesson Information/Assignment Task

Completed

LESSON 3
SUBJECT
_____

Lesson Information/Assignment Task

Completed

LESSON 4
SUBJECT
_____

Lesson Information/Assignment Task

Completed

LESSON 5
SUBJECT
_____

Lesson Information/Assignment Task

Completed

DATE / /

LESSON 1
SUBJECT

_____

Lesson Information/Assignment Task

Completed

LESSON 2
SUBJECT

_____

Lesson Information/Assignment Task

Completed

LESSON 3
SUBJECT

_____

Lesson Information/Assignment Task

Completed

LESSON 4
SUBJECT

_____

Lesson Information/Assignment Task

Completed

LESSON 5
SUBJECT

_____

Lesson Information/Assignment Task

Completed

DATE / /

LESSON 1
SUBJECT

_____

Lesson Information/Assignment Task

Completed

LESSON 2
SUBJECT

_____

Lesson Information/Assignment Task

Completed

LESSON 3
SUBJECT

_____

Lesson Information/Assignment Task

Completed

LESSON 4
SUBJECT

_____

Lesson Information/Assignment Task

Completed

LESSON 5
SUBJECT

_____

Lesson Information/Assignment Task

Completed

DATE / /

LESSON 1 SUBJECT _____	Lesson Information/Assignment Task
	Completed
LESSON 2 SUBJECT _____	Lesson Information/Assignment Task
	Completed
LESSON 3 SUBJECT _____	Lesson Information/Assignment Task
	Completed
LESSON 4 SUBJECT _____	Lesson Information/Assignment Task
	Completed
LESSON 5 SUBJECT _____	Lesson Information/Assignment Task
	Completed

DATE / /

LESSON 1 SUBJECT _____	Lesson Information/Assignment Task
	Completed
LESSON 2 SUBJECT _____	Lesson Information/Assignment Task
	Completed
LESSON 3 SUBJECT _____	Lesson Information/Assignment Task
	Completed
LESSON 4 SUBJECT _____	Lesson Information/Assignment Task
	Completed
LESSON 5 SUBJECT _____	Lesson Information/Assignment Task
	Completed

DATE ___ / ___ / ___

LESSON 1 SUBJECT _____	Lesson Information/Assignment Task
	Completed
LESSON 2 SUBJECT _____	Lesson Information/Assignment Task
	Completed
LESSON 3 SUBJECT _____	Lesson Information/Assignment Task
	Completed
LESSON 4 SUBJECT _____	Lesson Information/Assignment Task
	Completed
LESSON 5 SUBJECT _____	Lesson Information/Assignment Task
	Completed

DATE ___ / ___ / ___

LESSON 1 SUBJECT _____	Lesson Information/Assignment Task
	Completed
LESSON 2 SUBJECT _____	Lesson Information/Assignment Task
	Completed
LESSON 3 SUBJECT _____	Lesson Information/Assignment Task
	Completed
LESSON 4 SUBJECT _____	Lesson Information/Assignment Task
	Completed
LESSON 5 SUBJECT _____	Lesson Information/Assignment Task
	Completed

DATE / /

LESSON 1 SUBJECT _____	Lesson Information/Assignment Task
	Completed
LESSON 2 SUBJECT _____	Lesson Information/Assignment Task
	Completed
LESSON 3 SUBJECT _____	Lesson Information/Assignment Task
	Completed
LESSON 4 SUBJECT _____	Lesson Information/Assignment Task
	Completed
LESSON 5 SUBJECT _____	Lesson Information/Assignment Task
	Completed

DATE / /

LESSON 1 SUBJECT _____	Lesson Information/Assignment Task
	Completed
LESSON 2 SUBJECT _____	Lesson Information/Assignment Task
	Completed
LESSON 3 SUBJECT _____	Lesson Information/Assignment Task
	Completed
LESSON 4 SUBJECT _____	Lesson Information/Assignment Task
	Completed
LESSON 5 SUBJECT _____	Lesson Information/Assignment Task
	Completed

Progress Tracker

What are my current Top 5 Priorities I need to action?

1. _____

_____ Target Date to Complete / /

2. _____

_____ Target Date to Complete / /

3. _____

_____ Target Date to Complete / /

4. _____

_____ Target Date to Complete / /

5. _____

_____ Target Date to Complete / /

Other Notes or Details

DATE / /

LESSON 1 SUBJECT _____	Lesson Information/Assignment Task Completed
LESSON 2 SUBJECT _____	Lesson Information/Assignment Task Completed
LESSON 3 SUBJECT _____	Lesson Information/Assignment Task Completed
LESSON 4 SUBJECT _____	Lesson Information/Assignment Task Completed
LESSON 5 SUBJECT _____	Lesson Information/Assignment Task Completed

DATE / /

LESSON 1 SUBJECT _____	Lesson Information/Assignment Task Completed
LESSON 2 SUBJECT _____	Lesson Information/Assignment Task Completed
LESSON 3 SUBJECT _____	Lesson Information/Assignment Task Completed
LESSON 4 SUBJECT _____	Lesson Information/Assignment Task Completed
LESSON 5 SUBJECT _____	Lesson Information/Assignment Task Completed

DATE / /

LESSON 1
SUBJECT
_____

Lesson Information/Assignment Task

Completed

LESSON 2
SUBJECT
_____

Lesson Information/Assignment Task

Completed

LESSON 3
SUBJECT
_____

Lesson Information/Assignment Task

Completed

LESSON 4
SUBJECT
_____

Lesson Information/Assignment Task

Completed

LESSON 5
SUBJECT
_____

Lesson Information/Assignment Task

Completed

DATE / /

LESSON 1
SUBJECT
_____

Lesson Information/Assignment Task

Completed

LESSON 2
SUBJECT
_____

Lesson Information/Assignment Task

Completed

LESSON 3
SUBJECT
_____

Lesson Information/Assignment Task

Completed

LESSON 4
SUBJECT
_____

Lesson Information/Assignment Task

Completed

LESSON 5
SUBJECT
_____

Lesson Information/Assignment Task

Completed

DATE ___ / ___ / ___

LESSON 1 SUBJECT _____	Lesson Information/Assignment Task
	Completed
LESSON 2 SUBJECT _____	Lesson Information/Assignment Task
	Completed
LESSON 3 SUBJECT _____	Lesson Information/Assignment Task
	Completed
LESSON 4 SUBJECT _____	Lesson Information/Assignment Task
	Completed
LESSON 5 SUBJECT _____	Lesson Information/Assignment Task
	Completed

DATE ___ / ___ / ___

LESSON 1 SUBJECT _____	Lesson Information/Assignment Task
	Completed
LESSON 2 SUBJECT _____	Lesson Information/Assignment Task
	Completed
LESSON 3 SUBJECT _____	Lesson Information/Assignment Task
	Completed
LESSON 4 SUBJECT _____	Lesson Information/Assignment Task
	Completed
LESSON 5 SUBJECT _____	Lesson Information/Assignment Task
	Completed

DATE   /   /

LESSON 1 SUBJECT _____	Lesson Information/Assignment Task
	Completed
LESSON 2 SUBJECT _____	Lesson Information/Assignment Task
	Completed
LESSON 3 SUBJECT _____	Lesson Information/Assignment Task
	Completed
LESSON 4 SUBJECT _____	Lesson Information/Assignment Task
	Completed
LESSON 5 SUBJECT _____	Lesson Information/Assignment Task
	Completed

DATE   /   /

LESSON 1 SUBJECT _____	Lesson Information/Assignment Task
	Completed
LESSON 2 SUBJECT _____	Lesson Information/Assignment Task
	Completed
LESSON 3 SUBJECT _____	Lesson Information/Assignment Task
	Completed
LESSON 4 SUBJECT _____	Lesson Information/Assignment Task
	Completed
LESSON 5 SUBJECT _____	Lesson Information/Assignment Task
	Completed

The
HOMESCHOOL
Teacher's
Planner & Organizer

FOR THE ORGANIZED HOMESCHOOL TEACHER

STUDENT NAME

AGE

SCHOOL YEAR LEVEL

YEAR

The
HOMESCHOOL
Teacher's
Planner

SECTIONS

1. **12 Month Goals**

2. **Lesson Timetable**

3. **Attendance Log**

4. **Website & Resources Log**

5. **Important Dates**

6. **Weekly Lesson Planners**

7. **Major Assignment Log**

8. **Report Cards**

notes. _____

12 Month Goals

Write down the goals you wish to achieve over the next 12 months

PERSONAL GOALS

....
....
....
....

HEALTH & FITNESS GOALS

....
....
....
....

HOMESCHOOL GOALS

....
....
....
....
....

WEEKLY TIMETABLE

DATE COMMENCING: /   /

DAY	MONDAY	TUESDAY	WEDNESDAY
LESSON 1 *START TIME* :	Subject	Subject	Subject
LESSON 2 *START TIME* :			
LESSON 3 *START TIME* :			
LESSON 4 *START TIME* :			
LESSON 5 *START TIME* :			

Other information to note

THURSDAY	FRIDAY	NOTES
Subject	Subject	

WEEKEND

Lesson Timetable

Print and stick your timetable below

USE THIS BLANK SPACE OR THE TEMPLATE TIMETABLE PROVIDED

YOUR HOMESCHOOL
Lesson Timetable
Print and stick your timetable below

USE THIS BLANK SPACE OR THE TEMPLATE TIMETABLE PROVIDED

ATTENDANCE LOG

MONTH

DAYS											
1											
2											
3											
4											
5											
6											
7											
8											
9											
10											
11											
12											
13											
14											
15											
16											
17											
18											
19											
20											
21											
22											
23											
24											
25											
26											
27											
28											
29											
30											
31											
TOTAL											

TOTAL DAYS PRESENT =

TOTAL DAYS ABSENT =

IMPORTANT WEBSITE RESOURCES

Name	Website Address

Other Books or Resources

IMPORTANT DATES

Record the import Homeschool Year Dates

MONTH:

MONTH:

MONTH:

IMPORTANT DATES

Record the import Homeschool Year Dates

MONTH:

MONTH:

MONTH:

IMPORTANT DATES

Record the import Homeschool Year Dates

MONTH:

MONTH:

MONTH:

IMPORTANT DATES

Record the import Homeschool Year Dates

MONTH:

MONTH:

MONTH:

Progress Tracker

What are my current Top 5 Priorities I need to action?

1. _____

_____ Target Date to Complete __/__/__

2. _____

_____ Target Date to Complete __/__/__

3. _____

_____ Target Date to Complete __/__/__

4. _____

_____ Target Date to Complete __/__/__

5. _____

_____ Target Date to Complete __/__/__

Other Notes or Details

DATE / /

| LESSON 1 SUBJECT _____ | Lesson Information/Assignment Task |
| | Completed |

| LESSON 2 SUBJECT _____ | Lesson Information/Assignment Task |
| | Completed |

| LESSON 3 SUBJECT _____ | Lesson Information/Assignment Task |
| | Completed |

| LESSON 4 SUBJECT _____ | Lesson Information/Assignment Task |
| | Completed |

| LESSON 5 SUBJECT _____ | Lesson Information/Assignment Task |
| | Completed |

DATE / /

| LESSON 1 SUBJECT _____ | Lesson Information/Assignment Task |
| | Completed |

| LESSON 2 SUBJECT _____ | Lesson Information/Assignment Task |
| | Completed |

| LESSON 3 SUBJECT _____ | Lesson Information/Assignment Task |
| | Completed |

| LESSON 4 SUBJECT _____ | Lesson Information/Assignment Task |
| | Completed |

| LESSON 5 SUBJECT _____ | Lesson Information/Assignment Task |
| | Completed |

DATE   /   /

LESSON 1 SUBJECT _____	Lesson Information/Assignment Task
	Completed
LESSON 2 SUBJECT _____	Lesson Information/Assignment Task
	Completed
LESSON 3 SUBJECT _____	Lesson Information/Assignment Task
	Completed
LESSON 4 SUBJECT _____	Lesson Information/Assignment Task
	Completed
LESSON 5 SUBJECT _____	Lesson Information/Assignment Task
	Completed

DATE   /   /

LESSON 1 SUBJECT _____	Lesson Information/Assignment Task
	Completed
LESSON 2 SUBJECT _____	Lesson Information/Assignment Task
	Completed
LESSON 3 SUBJECT _____	Lesson Information/Assignment Task
	Completed
LESSON 4 SUBJECT _____	Lesson Information/Assignment Task
	Completed
LESSON 5 SUBJECT _____	Lesson Information/Assignment Task
	Completed

DATE / /

LESSON 1 SUBJECT _____	Lesson Information/Assignment Task
	Completed

LESSON 2 SUBJECT _____	Lesson Information/Assignment Task
	Completed

LESSON 3 SUBJECT _____	Lesson Information/Assignment Task
	Completed

LESSON 4 SUBJECT _____	Lesson Information/Assignment Task
	Completed

LESSON 5 SUBJECT _____	Lesson Information/Assignment Task
	Completed

DATE / /

LESSON 1 SUBJECT _____	Lesson Information/Assignment Task
	Completed

LESSON 2 SUBJECT _____	Lesson Information/Assignment Task
	Completed

LESSON 3 SUBJECT _____	Lesson Information/Assignment Task
	Completed

LESSON 4 SUBJECT _____	Lesson Information/Assignment Task
	Completed

LESSON 5 SUBJECT _____	Lesson Information/Assignment Task
	Completed

DATE / /

LESSON 1 SUBJECT _____	Lesson Information/Assignment Task Completed
LESSON 2 SUBJECT _____	Lesson Information/Assignment Task Completed
LESSON 3 SUBJECT _____	Lesson Information/Assignment Task Completed
LESSON 4 SUBJECT _____	Lesson Information/Assignment Task Completed
LESSON 5 SUBJECT _____	Lesson Information/Assignment Task Completed

DATE / /

LESSON 1 SUBJECT _____	Lesson Information/Assignment Task Completed
LESSON 2 SUBJECT _____	Lesson Information/Assignment Task Completed
LESSON 3 SUBJECT _____	Lesson Information/Assignment Task Completed
LESSON 4 SUBJECT _____	Lesson Information/Assignment Task Completed
LESSON 5 SUBJECT _____	Lesson Information/Assignment Task Completed

DATE / /

LESSON 1 SUBJECT _____	Lesson Information/Assignment Task
	Completed
LESSON 2 SUBJECT _____	Lesson Information/Assignment Task
	Completed
LESSON 3 SUBJECT _____	Lesson Information/Assignment Task
	Completed
LESSON 4 SUBJECT _____	Lesson Information/Assignment Task
	Completed
LESSON 5 SUBJECT _____	Lesson Information/Assignment Task
	Completed

DATE / /

LESSON 1 SUBJECT _____	Lesson Information/Assignment Task
	Completed
LESSON 2 SUBJECT _____	Lesson Information/Assignment Task
	Completed
LESSON 3 SUBJECT _____	Lesson Information/Assignment Task
	Completed
LESSON 4 SUBJECT _____	Lesson Information/Assignment Task
	Completed
LESSON 5 SUBJECT _____	Lesson Information/Assignment Task
	Completed

Progress Tracker

What are my current Top 5 Priorities I need to action?

1. _____

_____ Target Date to Complete   /   /

2. _____

_____ Target Date to Complete   /   /

3. _____

_____ Target Date to Complete   /   /

4. _____

_____ Target Date to Complete   /   /

5. _____

_____ Target Date to Complete   /   /

Other Notes or Details

DATE / /

| LESSON 1
SUBJECT
_____ | Lesson Information/Assignment Task

Completed |

| LESSON 2
SUBJECT
_____ | Lesson Information/Assignment Task

Completed |

| LESSON 3
SUBJECT
_____ | Lesson Information/Assignment Task

Completed |

| LESSON 4
SUBJECT
_____ | Lesson Information/Assignment Task

Completed |

| LESSON 5
SUBJECT
_____ | Lesson Information/Assignment Task

Completed |

DATE / /

| LESSON 1
SUBJECT
_____ | Lesson Information/Assignment Task

Completed |

| LESSON 2
SUBJECT
_____ | Lesson Information/Assignment Task

Completed |

| LESSON 3
SUBJECT
_____ | Lesson Information/Assignment Task

Completed |

| LESSON 4
SUBJECT
_____ | Lesson Information/Assignment Task

Completed |

| LESSON 5
SUBJECT
_____ | Lesson Information/Assignment Task

Completed |

DATE / /

LESSON 1 SUBJECT _____	Lesson Information/Assignment Task Completed
LESSON 2 SUBJECT _____	Lesson Information/Assignment Task Completed
LESSON 3 SUBJECT _____	Lesson Information/Assignment Task Completed
LESSON 4 SUBJECT _____	Lesson Information/Assignment Task Completed
LESSON 5 SUBJECT _____	Lesson Information/Assignment Task Completed

DATE / /

LESSON 1 SUBJECT _____	Lesson Information/Assignment Task Completed
LESSON 2 SUBJECT _____	Lesson Information/Assignment Task Completed
LESSON 3 SUBJECT _____	Lesson Information/Assignment Task Completed
LESSON 4 SUBJECT _____	Lesson Information/Assignment Task Completed
LESSON 5 SUBJECT _____	Lesson Information/Assignment Task Completed

DATE / /

LESSON 1 SUBJECT _____	Lesson Information/Assignment Task Completed
LESSON 2 SUBJECT _____	Lesson Information/Assignment Task Completed
LESSON 3 SUBJECT _____	Lesson Information/Assignment Task Completed
LESSON 4 SUBJECT _____	Lesson Information/Assignment Task Completed
LESSON 5 SUBJECT _____	Lesson Information/Assignment Task Completed

DATE / /

LESSON 1 SUBJECT _____	Lesson Information/Assignment Task Completed
LESSON 2 SUBJECT _____	Lesson Information/Assignment Task Completed
LESSON 3 SUBJECT _____	Lesson Information/Assignment Task Completed
LESSON 4 SUBJECT _____	Lesson Information/Assignment Task Completed
LESSON 5 SUBJECT _____	Lesson Information/Assignment Task Completeed

DATE ___ / ___ / ___

LESSON 1 SUBJECT _____	Lesson Information/Assignment Task Completed
LESSON 2 SUBJECT _____	Lesson Information/Assignment Task Completed
LESSON 3 SUBJECT _____	Lesson Information/Assignment Task Completed
LESSON 4 SUBJECT _____	Lesson Information/Assignment Task Completed
LESSON 5 SUBJECT _____	Lesson Information/Assignment Task Completed

DATE ___ / ___ / ___

LESSON 1 SUBJECT _____	Lesson Information/Assignment Task Completed
LESSON 2 SUBJECT _____	Lesson Information/Assignment Task Completed
LESSON 3 SUBJECT _____	Lesson Information/Assignment Task Completed
LESSON 4 SUBJECT _____	Lesson Information/Assignment Task Completed
LESSON 5 SUBJECT _____	Lesson Information/Assignment Task Completed

DATE / /

LESSON 1 SUBJECT _____	Lesson Information/Assignment Task Completed
LESSON 2 SUBJECT _____	Lesson Information/Assignment Task Completed
LESSON 3 SUBJECT _____	Lesson Information/Assignment Task Completed
LESSON 4 SUBJECT _____	Lesson Information/Assignment Task Completed
LESSON 5 SUBJECT _____	Lesson Information/Assignment Task Completed

DATE / /

LESSON 1 SUBJECT _____	Lesson Information/Assignment Task Completed
LESSON 2 SUBJECT _____	Lesson Information/Assignment Task Completed
LESSON 3 SUBJECT _____	Lesson Information/Assignment Task Completed
LESSON 4 SUBJECT _____	Lesson Information/Assignment Task Completed
LESSON 5 SUBJECT _____	Lesson Information/Assignment Task Completed

Progress Tracker

What are my current Top 5 Priorities I need to action?

1. _____

_____ Target Date to Complete / /

2. _____

_____ Target Date to Complete / /

3. _____

_____ Target Date to Complete / /

4. _____

_____ Target Date to Complete / /

5. _____

_____ Target Date to Complete / /

Other Notes or Details

DATE / /

LESSON 1 SUBJECT _____	Lesson Information/Assignment Task
	Completed
LESSON 2 SUBJECT _____	Lesson Information/Assignment Task
	Completed
LESSON 3 SUBJECT _____	Lesson Information/Assignment Task
	Completed
LESSON 4 SUBJECT _____	Lesson Information/Assignment Task
	Completed
LESSON 5 SUBJECT _____	Lesson Information/Assignment Task
	Completed

DATE / /

LESSON 1 SUBJECT _____	Lesson Information/Assignment Task
	Completed
LESSON 2 SUBJECT _____	Lesson Information/Assignment Task
	Completed
LESSON 3 SUBJECT _____	Lesson Information/Assignment Task
	Completed
LESSON 4 SUBJECT _____	Lesson Information/Assignment Task
	Completed
LESSON 5 SUBJECT _____	Lesson Information/Assignment Task
	Completed

DATE / /

LESSON 1 SUBJECT _____	Lesson Information/Assignment Task
	Completed
LESSON 2 SUBJECT _____	Lesson Information/Assignment Task
	Completed
LESSON 3 SUBJECT _____	Lesson Information/Assignment Task
	Completed
LESSON 4 SUBJECT _____	Lesson Information/Assignment Task
	Completed
LESSON 5 SUBJECT _____	Lesson Information/Assignment Task
	Completed

DATE / /

LESSON 1 SUBJECT _____	Lesson Information/Assignment Task
	Completed
LESSON 2 SUBJECT _____	Lesson Information/Assignment Task
	Completed
LESSON 3 SUBJECT _____	Lesson Information/Assignment Task
	Completed
LESSON 4 SUBJECT _____	Lesson Information/Assignment Task
	Completed
LESSON 5 SUBJECT _____	Lesson Information/Assignment Task
	Completed

DATE   /   /

LESSON 1 SUBJECT _____	Lesson Information/Assignment Task
	Completed

LESSON 2 SUBJECT _____	Lesson Information/Assignment Task
	Completed

LESSON 3 SUBJECT _____	Lesson Information/Assignment Task
	Completed

LESSON 4 SUBJECT _____	Lesson Information/Assignment Task
	Completed

LESSON 5 SUBJECT _____	Lesson Information/Assignment Task
	Completed

DATE   /   /

LESSON 1 SUBJECT _____	Lesson Information/Assignment Task
	Completed

LESSON 2 SUBJECT _____	Lesson Information/Assignment Task
	Completed

LESSON 3 SUBJECT _____	Lesson Information/Assignment Task
	Completed

LESSON 4 SUBJECT _____	Lesson Information/Assignment Task
	Completed

LESSON 5 SUBJECT _____	Lesson Information/Assignment Task
	Completed

DATE / /

LESSON 1
SUBJECT

_____

Lesson Information/Assignment Task

Completed

LESSON 2
SUBJECT

_____

Lesson Information/Assignment Task

Completed

LESSON 3
SUBJECT

_____

Lesson Information/Assignment Task

Completed

LESSON 4
SUBJECT

_____

Lesson Information/Assignment Task

Completed

LESSON 5
SUBJECT

_____

Lesson Information/Assignment Task

Completed

DATE / /

LESSON 1
SUBJECT

_____

Lesson Information/Assignment Task

Completed

LESSON 2
SUBJECT

_____

Lesson Information/Assignment Task

Completed

LESSON 3
SUBJECT

_____

Lesson Information/Assignment Task

Completed

LESSON 4
SUBJECT

_____

Lesson Information/Assignment Task

Completed

LESSON 5
SUBJECT

_____

Lesson Information/Assignment Task

Completed

DATE / /

LESSON 1 SUBJECT _____	Lesson Information/Assignment Task
	Completed

LESSON 2 SUBJECT _____	Lesson Information/Assignment Task
	Completed

LESSON 3 SUBJECT _____	Lesson Information/Assignment Task
	Completed

LESSON 4 SUBJECT _____	Lesson Information/Assignment Task
	Completed

LESSON 5 SUBJECT _____	Lesson Information/Assignment Task
	Completed

DATE / /

LESSON 1 SUBJECT _____	Lesson Information/Assignment Task
	Completed

LESSON 2 SUBJECT _____	Lesson Information/Assignment Task
	Completed

LESSON 3 SUBJECT _____	Lesson Information/Assignment Task
	Completed

LESSON 4 SUBJECT _____	Lesson Information/Assignment Task
	Completed

LESSON 5 SUBJECT _____	Lesson Information/Assignment Task
	Completed

Progress Tracker

What are my current Top 5 Priorities I need to action?

1. _____

_____ Target Date to Complete / /

2. _____

_____ Target Date to Complete / /

3. _____

_____ Target Date to Complete / /

4. _____

_____ Target Date to Complete / /

5. _____

_____ Target Date to Complete / /

Other Notes or Details

DATE / /

LESSON 1 SUBJECT _____	Lesson Information/Assignment Task
	Completed
LESSON 2 SUBJECT _____	Lesson Information/Assignment Task
	Completed
LESSON 3 SUBJECT _____	Lesson Information/Assignment Task
	Completed
LESSON 4 SUBJECT _____	Lesson Information/Assignment Task
	Completed
LESSON 5 SUBJECT _____	Lesson Information/Assignment Task
	Completed

DATE / /

LESSON 1 SUBJECT _____	Lesson Information/Assignment Task
	Completed
LESSON 2 SUBJECT _____	Lesson Information/Assignment Task
	Completed
LESSON 3 SUBJECT _____	Lesson Information/Assignment Task
	Completed
LESSON 4 SUBJECT _____	Lesson Information/Assignment Task
	Completed
LESSON 5 SUBJECT _____	Lesson Information/Assignment Task
	Completed

DATE   /   /

LESSON 1
SUBJECT

_____

Lesson Information/Assignment Task

Completed

LESSON 2
SUBJECT

_____

Lesson Information/Assignment Task

Completed

LESSON 3
SUBJECT

_____

Lesson Information/Assignment Task

Completed

LESSON 4
SUBJECT

_____

Lesson Information/Assignment Task

Completed

LESSON 5
SUBJECT

_____

Lesson Information/Assignment Task

Completed

DATE   /   /

LESSON 1
SUBJECT

_____

Lesson Information/Assignment Task

Completed

LESSON 2
SUBJECT

_____

Lesson Information/Assignment Task

Completed

LESSON 3
SUBJECT

_____

Lesson Information/Assignment Task

Completed

LESSON 4
SUBJECT

_____

Lesson Information/Assignment Task

Completed

LESSON 5
SUBJECT

_____

Lesson Information/Assignment Task

Completed

DATE / /

LESSON 1 SUBJECT _____	Lesson Information/Assignment Task Completed
LESSON 2 SUBJECT _____	Lesson Information/Assignment Task Completed
LESSON 3 SUBJECT _____	Lesson Information/Assignment Task Completed
LESSON 4 SUBJECT _____	Lesson Information/Assignment Task Completed
LESSON 5 SUBJECT _____	Lesson Information/Assignment Task Completed

DATE / /

LESSON 1 SUBJECT _____	Lesson Information/Assignment Task Completed
LESSON 2 SUBJECT _____	Lesson Information/Assignment Task Completed
LESSON 3 SUBJECT _____	Lesson Information/Assignment Task Completed
LESSON 4 SUBJECT _____	Lesson Information/Assignment Task Completed
LESSON 5 SUBJECT _____	Lesson Information/Assignment Task Completed

DATE / /

LESSON 1 SUBJECT _____	Lesson Information/Assignment Task
	Completed
LESSON 2 SUBJECT _____	Lesson Information/Assignment Task
	Completed
LESSON 3 SUBJECT _____	Lesson Information/Assignment Task
	Completed
LESSON 4 SUBJECT _____	Lesson Information/Assignment Task
	Completed
LESSON 5 SUBJECT _____	Lesson Information/Assignment Task
	Completed

DATE / /

LESSON 1 SUBJECT _____	Lesson Information/Assignment Task
	Completed
LESSON 2 SUBJECT _____	Lesson Information/Assignment Task
	Completed
LESSON 3 SUBJECT _____	Lesson Information/Assignment Task
	Completed
LESSON 4 SUBJECT _____	Lesson Information/Assignment Task
	Completed
LESSON 5 SUBJECT _____	Lesson Information/Assignment Task
	Completed

DATE / /

LESSON 1
SUBJECT
_____

Lesson Information/Assignment Task

Completed

LESSON 2
SUBJECT
_____

Lesson Information/Assignment Task

Completed

LESSON 3
SUBJECT
_____

Lesson Information/Assignment Task

Completed

LESSON 4
SUBJECT
_____

Lesson Information/Assignment Task

Completed

LESSON 5
SUBJECT
_____

Lesson Information/Assignment Task

Completed

DATE / /

LESSON 1
SUBJECT
_____

Lesson Information/Assignment Task

Completed

LESSON 2
SUBJECT
_____

Lesson Information/Assignment Task

Completed

LESSON 3
SUBJECT
_____

Lesson Information/Assignment Task

Completed

LESSON 4
SUBJECT
_____

Lesson Information/Assignment Task

Completed

LESSON 5
SUBJECT
_____

Lesson Information/Assignment Task

Completed

Progress Tracker

What are my current Top 5 Priorities I need to action?

1. _____

_____ Target Date to Complete __/__/__

2. _____

_____ Target Date to Complete __/__/__

3. _____

_____ Target Date to Complete __/__/__

4. _____

_____ Target Date to Complete __/__/__

5. _____

_____ Target Date to Complete __/__/__

Other Notes or Details

LESSON 1
SUBJECT

_____

Lesson Information/Assignment Task

Completed

LESSON 2
SUBJECT

_____

Lesson Information/Assignment Task

Completed

LESSON 3
SUBJECT

_____

Lesson Information/Assignment Task

Completed

LESSON 4
SUBJECT

_____

Lesson Information/Assignment Task

Completed

LESSON 5
SUBJECT

_____

Lesson Information/Assignment Task

Completed

DATE   /   /

LESSON 1
SUBJECT

_____

Lesson Information/Assignment Task

Completed

LESSON 2
SUBJECT

_____

Lesson Information/Assignment Task

Completed

LESSON 3
SUBJECT

_____

Lesson Information/Assignment Task

Completed

LESSON 4
SUBJECT

_____

Lesson Information/Assignment Task

Completed

LESSON 5
SUBJECT

_____

Lesson Information/Assignment Task

Completed

DATE ___/___/___

LESSON 1
SUBJECT
_____

Lesson Information/Assignment Task

Completed

LESSON 2
SUBJECT
_____

Lesson Information/Assignment Task

Completed

LESSON 3
SUBJECT
_____

Lesson Information/Assignment Task

Completed

LESSON 4
SUBJECT
_____

Lesson Information/Assignment Task

Completed

LESSON 5
SUBJECT
_____

Lesson Information/Assignment Task

Completed

DATE ___/___/___

LESSON 1
SUBJECT
_____

Lesson Information/Assignment Task

Completed

LESSON 2
SUBJECT
_____

Lesson Information/Assignment Task

Completed

LESSON 3
SUBJECT
_____

Lesson Information/Assignment Task

Completed

LESSON 4
SUBJECT
_____

Lesson Information/Assignment Task

Completed

LESSON 5
SUBJECT
_____

Lesson Information/Assignment Task

Completed

DATE / /

LESSON 1 SUBJECT _____	Lesson Information/Assignment Task
	Completed
LESSON 2 SUBJECT _____	Lesson Information/Assignment Task
	Completed
LESSON 3 SUBJECT _____	Lesson Information/Assignment Task
	Completed
LESSON 4 SUBJECT _____	Lesson Information/Assignment Task
	Completed
LESSON 5 SUBJECT _____	Lesson Information/Assignment Task
	Completed

DATE / /

LESSON 1 SUBJECT _____	Lesson Information/Assignment Task
	Completed
LESSON 2 SUBJECT _____	Lesson Information/Assignment Task
	Completed
LESSON 3 SUBJECT _____	Lesson Information/Assignment Task
	Completed
LESSON 4 SUBJECT _____	Lesson Information/Assignment Task
	Completed
LESSON 5 SUBJECT _____	Lesson Information/Assignment Task
	Completed

DATE / /

LESSON 1
SUBJECT

_____

Lesson Information/Assignment Task

Completed

LESSON 2
SUBJECT

_____

Lesson Information/Assignment Task

Completed

LESSON 3
SUBJECT

_____

Lesson Information/Assignment Task

Completed

LESSON 4
SUBJECT

_____

Lesson Information/Assignment Task

Completed

LESSON 5
SUBJECT

_____

Lesson Information/Assignment Task

Completed

DATE / /

LESSON 1
SUBJECT

_____

Lesson Information/Assignment Task

Completed

LESSON 2
SUBJECT

_____

Lesson Information/Assignment Task

Completed

LESSON 3
SUBJECT

_____

Lesson Information/Assignment Task

Completed

LESSON 4
SUBJECT

_____

Lesson Information/Assignment Task

Completed

LESSON 5
SUBJECT

_____

Lesson Information/Assignment Task

Completed

DATE   /   /

LESSON 1
SUBJECT

_____

Lesson Information/Assignment Task

Completed

LESSON 2
SUBJECT

_____

Lesson Information/Assignment Task

Completed

LESSON 3
SUBJECT

_____

Lesson Information/Assignment Task

Completed

LESSON 4
SUBJECT

_____

Lesson Information/Assignment Task

Completed

LESSON 5
SUBJECT

_____

Lesson Information/Assignment Task

Completed

DATE   /   /

LESSON 1
SUBJECT

_____

Lesson Information/Assignment Task

Completed

LESSON 2
SUBJECT

_____

Lesson Information/Assignment Task

Completed

LESSON 3
SUBJECT

_____

Lesson Information/Assignment Task

Completed

LESSON 4
SUBJECT

_____

Lesson Information/Assignment Task

Completed

LESSON 5
SUBJECT

_____

Lesson Information/Assignment Task

Completeted

Progress Tracker

What are my current Top 5 Priorities I need to action?

1. _____

_____ Target Date to Complete __/__/__

2. _____

_____ Target Date to Complete __/__/__

3. _____

_____ Target Date to Complete __/__/__

4. _____

_____ Target Date to Complete __/__/__

5. _____

_____ Target Date to Complete __/__/__

Other Notes or Details

DATE   /   /

LESSON 1
SUBJECT

_____

Lesson Information/Assignment Task

Completed

LESSON 2
SUBJECT

_____

Lesson Information/Assignment Task

Completed

LESSON 3
SUBJECT

_____

Lesson Information/Assignment Task

Completed

LESSON 4
SUBJECT

_____

Lesson Information/Assignment Task

Completed

LESSON 5
SUBJECT

_____

Lesson Information/Assignment Task

Completed

DATE   /   /

LESSON 1
SUBJECT

_____

Lesson Information/Assignment Task

Completed

LESSON 2
SUBJECT

_____

Lesson Information/Assignment Task

Completed

LESSON 3
SUBJECT

_____

Lesson Information/Assignment Task

Completed

LESSON 4
SUBJECT

_____

Lesson Information/Assignment Task

Completed

LESSON 5
SUBJECT

_____

Lesson Information/Assignment Task

Completed

DATE / /

LESSON 1 SUBJECT _____	Lesson Information/Assignment Task Completed
LESSON 2 SUBJECT _____	Lesson Information/Assignment Task Completed
LESSON 3 SUBJECT _____	Lesson Information/Assignment Task Completed
LESSON 4 SUBJECT _____	Lesson Information/Assignment Task Completed
LESSON 5 SUBJECT _____	Lesson Information/Assignment Task Completed

DATE / /

LESSON 1 SUBJECT _____	Lesson Information/Assignment Task Completed
LESSON 2 SUBJECT _____	Lesson Information/Assignment Task Completed
LESSON 3 SUBJECT _____	Lesson Information/Assignment Task Completed
LESSON 4 SUBJECT _____	Lesson Information/Assignment Task Completed
LESSON 5 SUBJECT _____	Lesson Information/Assignment Task Completed

DATE   /   /

LESSON 1
SUBJECT
_____

Lesson Information/Assignment Task

Completed

LESSON 2
SUBJECT
_____

Lesson Information/Assignment Task

Completed

LESSON 3
SUBJECT
_____

Lesson Information/Assignment Task

Completed

LESSON 4
SUBJECT
_____

Lesson Information/Assignment Task

Completed

LESSON 5
SUBJECT
_____

Lesson Information/Assignment Task

Completed

DATE   /   /

LESSON 1
SUBJECT
_____

Lesson Information/Assignment Task

Completed

LESSON 2
SUBJECT
_____

Lesson Information/Assignment Task

Completed

LESSON 3
SUBJECT
_____

Lesson Information/Assignment Task

Completed

LESSON 4
SUBJECT
_____

Lesson Information/Assignment Task

Completed

LESSON 5
SUBJECT
_____

Lesson Information/Assignment Task

Completed

DATE / /

LESSON 1 SUBJECT _____	Lesson Information/Assignment Task Completed
LESSON 2 SUBJECT _____	Lesson Information/Assignment Task Completed
LESSON 3 SUBJECT _____	Lesson Information/Assignment Task Completed
LESSON 4 SUBJECT _____	Lesson Information/Assignment Task Completed
LESSON 5 SUBJECT _____	Lesson Information/Assignment Task Completed

DATE / /

LESSON 1 SUBJECT _____	Lesson Information/Assignment Task Completed
LESSON 2 SUBJECT _____	Lesson Information/Assignment Task Completed
LESSON 3 SUBJECT _____	Lesson Information/Assignment Task Completed
LESSON 4 SUBJECT _____	Lesson Information/Assignment Task Completed
LESSON 5 SUBJECT _____	Lesson Information/Assignment Task Completed

DATE / /

LESSON 1 SUBJECT _____	Lesson Information/Assignment Task
	Completed
LESSON 2 SUBJECT _____	Lesson Information/Assignment Task
	Completed
LESSON 3 SUBJECT _____	Lesson Information/Assignment Task
	Completed
LESSON 4 SUBJECT _____	Lesson Information/Assignment Task
	Completed
LESSON 5 SUBJECT _____	Lesson Information/Assignment Task
	Completed

DATE / /

LESSON 1 SUBJECT _____	Lesson Information/Assignment Task
	Completed
LESSON 2 SUBJECT _____	Lesson Information/Assignment Task
	Completed
LESSON 3 SUBJECT _____	Lesson Information/Assignment Task
	Completed
LESSON 4 SUBJECT _____	Lesson Information/Assignment Task
	Completed
LESSON 5 SUBJECT _____	Lesson Information/Assignment Task
	Completed

Progress Tracker

What are my current Top 5 Priorities I need to action?

1. _____

_____ Target Date to Complete ___ / ___ / ___

2. _____

_____ Target Date to Complete ___ / ___ / ___

3. _____

_____ Target Date to Complete ___ / ___ / ___

4. _____

_____ Target Date to Complete ___ / ___ / ___

5. _____

_____ Target Date to Complete ___ / ___ / ___

Other Notes or Details

DATE   /   /

LESSON 1
SUBJECT

_____

Lesson Information/Assignment Task

Completed

LESSON 2
SUBJECT

_____

Lesson Information/Assignment Task

Completed

LESSON 3
SUBJECT

_____

Lesson Information/Assignment Task

Completed

LESSON 4
SUBJECT

_____

Lesson Information/Assignment Task

Completed

LESSON 5
SUBJECT

_____

Lesson Information/Assignment Task

Completed

DATE   /   /

LESSON 1
SUBJECT

_____

Lesson Information/Assignment Task

Completed

LESSON 2
SUBJECT

_____

Lesson Information/Assignment Task

Completed

LESSON 3
SUBJECT

_____

Lesson Information/Assignment Task

Completed

LESSON 4
SUBJECT

_____

Lesson Information/Assignment Task

Completed

LESSON 5
SUBJECT

_____

Lesson Information/Assignment Task

Completed

DATE   /   /

LESSON 1
SUBJECT
_____

Lesson Information/Assignment Task

Completed

LESSON 2
SUBJECT
_____

Lesson Information/Assignment Task

Completed

LESSON 3
SUBJECT
_____

Lesson Information/Assignment Task

Completed

LESSON 4
SUBJECT
_____

Lesson Information/Assignment Task

Completed

LESSON 5
SUBJECT
_____

Lesson Information/Assignment Task

Completed

DATE   /   /

LESSON 1
SUBJECT
_____

Lesson Information/Assignment Task

Completed

LESSON 2
SUBJECT
_____

Lesson Information/Assignment Task

Completed

LESSON 3
SUBJECT
_____

Lesson Information/Assignment Task

Completed

LESSON 4
SUBJECT
_____

Lesson Information/Assignment Task

Completed

LESSON 5
SUBJECT
_____

Lesson Information/Assignment Task

Completed

DATE   /   /

LESSON 1
SUBJECT

_____

Lesson Information/Assignment Task

Completed

LESSON 2
SUBJECT

_____

Lesson Information/Assignment Task

Completed

LESSON 3
SUBJECT

_____

Lesson Information/Assignment Task

Completed

LESSON 4
SUBJECT

_____

Lesson Information/Assignment Task

Completed

LESSON 5
SUBJECT

_____

Lesson Information/Assignment Task

Completed

DATE   /   /

LESSON 1
SUBJECT

_____

Lesson Information/Assignment Task

Completed

LESSON 2
SUBJECT

_____

Lesson Information/Assignment Task

Completed

LESSON 3
SUBJECT

_____

Lesson Information/Assignment Task

Completed

LESSON 4
SUBJECT

_____

Lesson Information/Assignment Task

Completed

LESSON 5
SUBJECT

_____

Lesson Information/Assignment Task

Completed

DATE ___/___/___

LESSON 1 SUBJECT _____	Lesson Information/Assignment Task Completed
LESSON 2 SUBJECT _____	Lesson Information/Assignment Task Completed
LESSON 3 SUBJECT _____	Lesson Information/Assignment Task Completed
LESSON 4 SUBJECT _____	Lesson Information/Assignment Task Completed
LESSON 5 SUBJECT _____	Lesson Information/Assignment Task Completed

DATE ___/___/___

LESSON 1 SUBJECT _____	Lesson Information/Assignment Task Completed
LESSON 2 SUBJECT _____	Lesson Information/Assignment Task Completed
LESSON 3 SUBJECT _____	Lesson Information/Assignment Task Completed
LESSON 4 SUBJECT _____	Lesson Information/Assignment Task Completed
LESSON 5 SUBJECT _____	Lesson Information/Assignment Task Completed

DATE / /

| **LESSON 1** SUBJECT _____ | Lesson Information/Assignment Task Completed |

| **LESSON 2** SUBJECT _____ | Lesson Information/Assignment Task Completed |

| **LESSON 3** SUBJECT _____ | Lesson Information/Assignment Task Completed |

| **LESSON 4** SUBJECT _____ | Lesson Information/Assignment Task Completed |

| **LESSON 5** SUBJECT _____ | Lesson Information/Assignment Task Completed |

DATE / /

| **LESSON 1** SUBJECT _____ | Lesson Information/Assignment Task Completed |

| **LESSON 2** SUBJECT _____ | Lesson Information/Assignment Task Completed |

| **LESSON 3** SUBJECT _____ | Lesson Information/Assignment Task Completed |

| **LESSON 4** SUBJECT _____ | Lesson Information/Assignment Task Completed |

| **LESSON 5** SUBJECT _____ | Lesson Information/Assignment Task Completed |

Progress Tracker

What are my current Top 5 Priorities I need to action?

1. _____

_____ Target Date to Complete   /   /

2. _____

_____ Target Date to Complete   /   /

3. _____

_____ Target Date to Complete   /   /

4. _____

_____ Target Date to Complete   /   /

5. _____

_____ Target Date to Complete   /   /

Other Notes or Details

DATE ___ / ___ / ___

LESSON 1
SUBJECT
_____

Lesson Information/Assignment Task

Completed

LESSON 2
SUBJECT
_____

Lesson Information/Assignment Task

Completed

LESSON 3
SUBJECT
_____

Lesson Information/Assignment Task

Completed

LESSON 4
SUBJECT
_____

Lesson Information/Assignment Task

Completed

LESSON 5
SUBJECT
_____

Lesson Information/Assignment Task

Completed

DATE ___ / ___ / ___

LESSON 1
SUBJECT
_____

Lesson Information/Assignment Task

Completed

LESSON 2
SUBJECT
_____

Lesson Information/Assignment Task

Completed

LESSON 3
SUBJECT
_____

Lesson Information/Assignment Task

Completed

LESSON 4
SUBJECT
_____

Lesson Information/Assignment Task

Completed

LESSON 5
SUBJECT
_____

Lesson Information/Assignment Task

Completed

DATE / /

LESSON 1 SUBJECT _____	Lesson Information/Assignment Task Completed
LESSON 2 SUBJECT _____	Lesson Information/Assignment Task Completed
LESSON 3 SUBJECT _____	Lesson Information/Assignment Task Completed
LESSON 4 SUBJECT _____	Lesson Information/Assignment Task Completed
LESSON 5 SUBJECT _____	Lesson Information/Assignment Task Completed

DATE / /

LESSON 1 SUBJECT _____	Lesson Information/Assignment Task Completed
LESSON 2 SUBJECT _____	Lesson Information/Assignment Task Completed
LESSON 3 SUBJECT _____	Lesson Information/Assignment Task Completed
LESSON 4 SUBJECT _____	Lesson Information/Assignment Task Completed
LESSON 5 SUBJECT _____	Lesson Information/Assignment Task Completed

DATE   /   /

LESSON 1 SUBJECT _____	Lesson Information/Assignment Task Completed
LESSON 2 SUBJECT _____	Lesson Information/Assignment Task Completed
LESSON 3 SUBJECT _____	Lesson Information/Assignment Task Completed
LESSON 4 SUBJECT _____	Lesson Information/Assignment Task Completed
LESSON 5 SUBJECT _____	Lesson Information/Assignment Task Completed

DATE   /   /

LESSON 1 SUBJECT _____	Lesson Information/Assignment Task Completed
LESSON 2 SUBJECT _____	Lesson Information/Assignment Task Completed
LESSON 3 SUBJECT _____	Lesson Information/Assignment Task Completed
LESSON 4 SUBJECT _____	Lesson Information/Assignment Task Completed
LESSON 5 SUBJECT _____	Lesson Information/Assignment Task Completed

DATE / /

LESSON 1 SUBJECT _____	Lesson Information/Assignment Task Completed
LESSON 2 SUBJECT _____	Lesson Information/Assignment Task Completed
LESSON 3 SUBJECT _____	Lesson Information/Assignment Task Completed
LESSON 4 SUBJECT _____	Lesson Information/Assignment Task Completed
LESSON 5 SUBJECT _____	Lesson Information/Assignment Task Completed

DATE / /

LESSON 1 SUBJECT _____	Lesson Information/Assignment Task Completed
LESSON 2 SUBJECT _____	Lesson Information/Assignment Task Completed
LESSON 3 SUBJECT _____	Lesson Information/Assignment Task Completed
LESSON 4 SUBJECT _____	Lesson Information/Assignment Task Completed
LESSON 5 SUBJECT _____	Lesson Information/Assignment Task Completed

DATE / /

| **LESSON 1**
SUBJECT
_____ | Lesson Information/Assignment Task

Completed |

| **LESSON 2**
SUBJECT
_____ | Lesson Information/Assignment Task

Completed |

| **LESSON 3**
SUBJECT
_____ | Lesson Information/Assignment Task

Completed |

| **LESSON 4**
SUBJECT
_____ | Lesson Information/Assignment Task

Completed |

| **LESSON 5**
SUBJECT
_____ | Lesson Information/Assignment Task

Completed |

DATE / /

| **LESSON 1**
SUBJECT
_____ | Lesson Information/Assignment Task

Completed |

| **LESSON 2**
SUBJECT
_____ | Lesson Information/Assignment Task

Completed |

| **LESSON 3**
SUBJECT
_____ | Lesson Information/Assignment Task

Completed |

| **LESSON 4**
SUBJECT
_____ | Lesson Information/Assignment Task

Completed |

| **LESSON 5**
SUBJECT
_____ | Lesson Information/Assignment Task

Completed |

Progress Tracker

What are my current Top 5 Priorities I need to action?

1. _____

_____ Target Date to Complete __ / __ / __

2. _____

_____ Target Date to Complete __ / __ / __

3. _____

_____ Target Date to Complete __ / __ / __

4. _____

_____ Target Date to Complete __ / __ / __

5. _____

_____ Target Date to Complete __ / __ / __

Other Notes or Details

DATE / /

LESSON 1 SUBJECT _____	Lesson Information/Assignment Task Completed
LESSON 2 SUBJECT _____	Lesson Information/Assignment Task Completed
LESSON 3 SUBJECT _____	Lesson Information/Assignment Task Completed
LESSON 4 SUBJECT _____	Lesson Information/Assignment Task Completed
LESSON 5 SUBJECT _____	Lesson Information/Assignment Task Completed

DATE / /

LESSON 1 SUBJECT _____	Lesson Information/Assignment Task Completed
LESSON 2 SUBJECT _____	Lesson Information/Assignment Task Completed
LESSON 3 SUBJECT _____	Lesson Information/Assignment Task Completed
LESSON 4 SUBJECT _____	Lesson Information/Assignment Task Completed
LESSON 5 SUBJECT _____	Lesson Information/Assignment Task Completed

DATE / /

LESSON 1 SUBJECT _____	Lesson Information/Assignment Task Completed
LESSON 2 SUBJECT _____	Lesson Information/Assignment Task Completed
LESSON 3 SUBJECT _____	Lesson Information/Assignment Task Completed
LESSON 4 SUBJECT _____	Lesson Information/Assignment Task Completed
LESSON 5 SUBJECT _____	Lesson Information/Assignment Task Completed

DATE / /

LESSON 1 SUBJECT _____	Lesson Information/Assignment Task Completed
LESSON 2 SUBJECT _____	Lesson Information/Assignment Task Completed
LESSON 3 SUBJECT _____	Lesson Information/Assignment Task Completed
LESSON 4 SUBJECT _____	Lesson Information/Assignment Task Completed
LESSON 5 SUBJECT _____	Lesson Information/Assignment Task Completed

DATE / /

LESSON 1 SUBJECT _____	Lesson Information/Assignment Task Completed
LESSON 2 SUBJECT _____	Lesson Information/Assignment Task Completed
LESSON 3 SUBJECT _____	Lesson Information/Assignment Task Completed
LESSON 4 SUBJECT _____	Lesson Information/Assignment Task Completed
LESSON 5 SUBJECT _____	Lesson Information/Assignment Task Completed

DATE / /

LESSON 1 SUBJECT _____	Lesson Information/Assignment Task Completed
LESSON 2 SUBJECT _____	Lesson Information/Assignment Task Completed
LESSON 3 SUBJECT _____	Lesson Information/Assignment Task Completed
LESSON 4 SUBJECT _____	Lesson Information/Assignment Task Completed
LESSON 5 SUBJECT _____	Lesson Information/Assignment Task Completed

DATE / /

LESSON 1 SUBJECT _____	Lesson Information/Assignment Task Completed
LESSON 2 SUBJECT _____	Lesson Information/Assignment Task Completed
LESSON 3 SUBJECT _____	Lesson Information/Assignment Task Completed
LESSON 4 SUBJECT _____	Lesson Information/Assignment Task Completed
LESSON 5 SUBJECT _____	Lesson Information/Assignment Task Completed

DATE / /

LESSON 1 SUBJECT _____	Lesson Information/Assignment Task Completed
LESSON 2 SUBJECT _____	Lesson Information/Assignment Task Completed
LESSON 3 SUBJECT _____	Lesson Information/Assignment Task Completed
LESSON 4 SUBJECT _____	Lesson Information/Assignment Task Completed
LESSON 5 SUBJECT _____	Lesson Information/Assignment Task Completed

DATE / /

LESSON 1
SUBJECT

_____

Lesson Information/Assignment Task

Completed

LESSON 2
SUBJECT

_____

Lesson Information/Assignment Task

Completed

LESSON 3
SUBJECT

_____

Lesson Information/Assignment Task

Completed

LESSON 4
SUBJECT

_____

Lesson Information/Assignment Task

Completed

LESSON 5
SUBJECT

_____

Lesson Information/Assignment Task

Completed

DATE / /

LESSON 1
SUBJECT

_____

Lesson Information/Assignment Task

Completed

LESSON 2
SUBJECT

_____

Lesson Information/Assignment Task

Completed

LESSON 3
SUBJECT

_____

Lesson Information/Assignment Task

Completed

LESSON 4
SUBJECT

_____

Lesson Information/Assignment Task

Completed

LESSON 5
SUBJECT

_____

Lesson Information/Assignment Task

Completed

Progress Tracker

What are my current Top 5 Priorities I need to action?

1. _____

_____ Target Date to Complete   /   /

2. _____

_____ Target Date to Complete   /   /

3. _____

_____ Target Date to Complete   /   /

4. _____

_____ Target Date to Complete   /   /

5. _____

_____ Target Date to Complete   /   /

Other Notes or Details

DATE / /

| LESSON 1 SUBJECT _____ | Lesson Information/Assignment Task |
| | Completed |

| LESSON 2 SUBJECT _____ | Lesson Information/Assignment Task |
| | Completed |

| LESSON 3 SUBJECT _____ | Lesson Information/Assignment Task |
| | Completed |

| LESSON 4 SUBJECT _____ | Lesson Information/Assignment Task |
| | Completed |

| LESSON 5 SUBJECT _____ | Lesson Information/Assignment Task |
| | Completed |

DATE / /

| LESSON 1 SUBJECT _____ | Lesson Information/Assignment Task |
| | Completed |

| LESSON 2 SUBJECT _____ | Lesson Information/Assignment Task |
| | Completed |

| LESSON 3 SUBJECT _____ | Lesson Information/Assignment Task |
| | Completed |

| LESSON 4 SUBJECT _____ | Lesson Information/Assignment Task |
| | Completed |

| LESSON 5 SUBJECT _____ | Lesson Information/Assignment Task |
| | Completed |

DATE __ / __ / __

LESSON 1
SUBJECT

_____

Lesson Information/Assignment Task

Completed

LESSON 2
SUBJECT

_____

Lesson Information/Assignment Task

Completed

LESSON 3
SUBJECT

_____

Lesson Information/Assignment Task

Completed

LESSON 4
SUBJECT

_____

Lesson Information/Assignment Task

Completed

LESSON 5
SUBJECT

_____

Lesson Information/Assignment Task

Completed

DATE __ / __ / __

LESSON 1
SUBJECT

_____

Lesson Information/Assignment Task

Completed

LESSON 2
SUBJECT

_____

Lesson Information/Assignment Task

Completed

LESSON 3
SUBJECT

_____

Lesson Information/Assignment Task

Completed

LESSON 4
SUBJECT

_____

Lesson Information/Assignment Task

Completed

LESSON 5
SUBJECT

_____

Lesson Information/Assignment Task

Completed

DATE / /

LESSON 1 SUBJECT _____	Lesson Information/Assignment Task
	Completed
LESSON 2 SUBJECT _____	Lesson Information/Assignment Task
	Completed
LESSON 3 SUBJECT _____	Lesson Information/Assignment Task
	Completed
LESSON 4 SUBJECT _____	Lesson Information/Assignment Task
	Completed
LESSON 5 SUBJECT _____	Lesson Information/Assignment Task
	Completed

DATE / /

LESSON 1 SUBJECT _____	Lesson Information/Assignment Task
	Completed
LESSON 2 SUBJECT _____	Lesson Information/Assignment Task
	Completed
LESSON 3 SUBJECT _____	Lesson Information/Assignment Task
	Completed
LESSON 4 SUBJECT _____	Lesson Information/Assignment Task
	Completed
LESSON 5 SUBJECT _____	Lesson Information/Assignment Task
	Completed

DATE / /

LESSON 1 SUBJECT _____	Lesson Information/Assignment Task
	Completed
LESSON 2 SUBJECT _____	Lesson Information/Assignment Task
	Completed
LESSON 3 SUBJECT _____	Lesson Information/Assignment Task
	Completed
LESSON 4 SUBJECT _____	Lesson Information/Assignment Task
	Completed
LESSON 5 SUBJECT _____	Lesson Information/Assignment Task
	Completed

DATE / /

LESSON 1 SUBJECT _____	Lesson Information/Assignment Task
	Completed
LESSON 2 SUBJECT _____	Lesson Information/Assignment Task
	Completed
LESSON 3 SUBJECT _____	Lesson Information/Assignment Task
	Completed
LESSON 4 SUBJECT _____	Lesson Information/Assignment Task
	Completed
LESSON 5 SUBJECT _____	Lesson Information/Assignment Task
	Completed

DATE   /   /

LESSON 1
SUBJECT
_____

Lesson Information/Assignment Task

Completed

LESSON 2
SUBJECT
_____

Lesson Information/Assignment Task

Completed

LESSON 3
SUBJECT
_____

Lesson Information/Assignment Task

Completed

LESSON 4
SUBJECT
_____

Lesson Information/Assignment Task

Completed

LESSON 5
SUBJECT
_____

Lesson Information/Assignment Task

Completed

DATE   /   /

LESSON 1
SUBJECT
_____

Lesson Information/Assignment Task

Completed

LESSON 2
SUBJECT
_____

Lesson Information/Assignment Task

Completed

LESSON 3
SUBJECT
_____

Lesson Information/Assignment Task

Completed

LESSON 4
SUBJECT
_____

Lesson Information/Assignment Task

Completed

LESSON 5
SUBJECT
_____

Lesson Information/Assignment Task

Completed

Progress Tracker

What are my current Top 5 Priorities I need to action?

1. _____

_____ Target Date to Complete / /

2. _____

_____ Target Date to Complete / /

3. _____

_____ Target Date to Complete / /

4. _____

_____ Target Date to Complete / /

5. _____

_____ Target Date to Complete / /

Other Notes or Details

DATE / /

LESSON 1 SUBJECT _____	Lesson Information/Assignment Task
	Completed
LESSON 2 SUBJECT _____	Lesson Information/Assignment Task
	Completed
LESSON 3 SUBJECT _____	Lesson Information/Assignment Task
	Completed
LESSON 4 SUBJECT _____	Lesson Information/Assignment Task
	Completed
LESSON 5 SUBJECT _____	Lesson Information/Assignment Task
	Completed

DATE / /

LESSON 1 SUBJECT _____	Lesson Information/Assignment Task
	Completed
LESSON 2 SUBJECT _____	Lesson Information/Assignment Task
	Completed
LESSON 3 SUBJECT _____	Lesson Information/Assignment Task
	Completed
LESSON 4 SUBJECT _____	Lesson Information/Assignment Task
	Completed
LESSON 5 SUBJECT _____	Lesson Information/Assignment Task
	Completed

DATE / /

LESSON 1 SUBJECT	Lesson Information/Assignment Task
_____	Completed

LESSON 2 SUBJECT	Lesson Information/Assignment Task
_____	Completed

LESSON 3 SUBJECT	Lesson Information/Assignment Task
_____	Completed

LESSON 4 SUBJECT	Lesson Information/Assignment Task
_____	Completed

LESSON 5 SUBJECT	Lesson Information/Assignment Task
_____	Completed

DATE / /

LESSON 1 SUBJECT	Lesson Information/Assignment Task
_____	Completed

LESSON 2 SUBJECT	Lesson Information/Assignment Task
_____	Completed

LESSON 3 SUBJECT	Lesson Information/Assignment Task
_____	Completed

LESSON 4 SUBJECT	Lesson Information/Assignment Task
_____	Completed

LESSON 5 SUBJECT	Lesson Information/Assignment Task
_____	Completed

DATE / /

LESSON 1
SUBJECT
_____

Lesson Information/Assignment Task

Completed

LESSON 2
SUBJECT
_____

Lesson Information/Assignment Task

Completed

LESSON 3
SUBJECT
_____

Lesson Information/Assignment Task

Completed

LESSON 4
SUBJECT
_____

Lesson Information/Assignment Task

Completed

LESSON 5
SUBJECT
_____

Lesson Information/Assignment Task

Completed

DATE / /

LESSON 1
SUBJECT
_____

Lesson Information/Assignment Task

Completed

LESSON 2
SUBJECT
_____

Lesson Information/Assignment Task

Completed

LESSON 3
SUBJECT
_____

Lesson Information/Assignment Task

Completed

LESSON 4
SUBJECT
_____

Lesson Information/Assignment Task

Completed

LESSON 5
SUBJECT
_____

Lesson Information/Assignment Task

Completed

DATE ___ / ___ / ___

LESSON 1 SUBJECT _____	Lesson Information/Assignment Task
	Completed

LESSON 2 SUBJECT _____	Lesson Information/Assignment Task
	Completed

LESSON 3 SUBJECT _____	Lesson Information/Assignment Task
	Completed

LESSON 4 SUBJECT _____	Lesson Information/Assignment Task
	Completed

LESSON 5 SUBJECT _____	Lesson Information/Assignment Task
	Completed

DATE ___ / ___ / ___

LESSON 1 SUBJECT _____	Lesson Information/Assignment Task
	Completed

LESSON 2 SUBJECT _____	Lesson Information/Assignment Task
	Completed

LESSON 3 SUBJECT _____	Lesson Information/Assignment Task
	Completed

LESSON 4 SUBJECT _____	Lesson Information/Assignment Task
	Completed

LESSON 5 SUBJECT _____	Lesson Information/Assignment Task
	Completed

DATE / /

LESSON 1 SUBJECT _____	Lesson Information/Assignment Task Completed
LESSON 2 SUBJECT _____	Lesson Information/Assignment Task Completed
LESSON 3 SUBJECT _____	Lesson Information/Assignment Task Completed
LESSON 4 SUBJECT _____	Lesson Information/Assignment Task Completed
LESSON 5 SUBJECT _____	Lesson Information/Assignment Task Completed

DATE / /

LESSON 1 SUBJECT _____	Lesson Information/Assignment Task Completed
LESSON 2 SUBJECT _____	Lesson Information/Assignment Task Completed
LESSON 3 SUBJECT _____	Lesson Information/Assignment Task Completed
LESSON 4 SUBJECT _____	Lesson Information/Assignment Task Completed
LESSON 5 SUBJECT _____	Lesson Information/Assignment Task Completed

Progress Tracker

What are my current Top 5 Priorities I need to action?

1. _____

_____ Target Date to Complete / /

2. _____

_____ Target Date to Complete / /

3. _____

_____ Target Date to Complete / /

4. _____

_____ Target Date to Complete / /

5. _____

_____ Target Date to Complete / /

Other Notes or Details

DATE   /   /

LESSON 1
SUBJECT
_____

Lesson Information/Assignment Task

Completed

LESSON 2
SUBJECT
_____

Lesson Information/Assignment Task

Completed

LESSON 3
SUBJECT
_____

Lesson Information/Assignment Task

Completed

LESSON 4
SUBJECT
_____

Lesson Information/Assignment Task

Completed

LESSON 5
SUBJECT
_____

Lesson Information/Assignment Task

Completed

DATE   /   /

LESSON 1
SUBJECT
_____

Lesson Information/Assignment Task

Completed

LESSON 2
SUBJECT
_____

Lesson Information/Assignment Task

Completed

LESSON 3
SUBJECT
_____

Lesson Information/Assignment Task

Completed

LESSON 4
SUBJECT
_____

Lesson Information/Assignment Task

Completed

LESSON 5
SUBJECT
_____

Lesson Information/Assignment Task

Completed

DATE / /

LESSON 1
SUBJECT

_____

Lesson Information/Assignment Task

Completed

LESSON 2
SUBJECT

_____

Lesson Information/Assignment Task

Completed

LESSON 3
SUBJECT

_____

Lesson Information/Assignment Task

Completed

LESSON 4
SUBJECT

_____

Lesson Information/Assignment Task

Completed

LESSON 5
SUBJECT

_____

Lesson Information/Assignment Task

Completed

DATE / /

LESSON 1
SUBJECT

_____

Lesson Information/Assignment Task

Completed

LESSON 2
SUBJECT

_____

Lesson Information/Assignment Task

Completed

LESSON 3
SUBJECT

_____

Lesson Information/Assignment Task

Completed

LESSON 4
SUBJECT

_____

Lesson Information/Assignment Task

Completed

LESSON 5
SUBJECT

_____

Lesson Information/Assignment Task

Completed

DATE / /

| **LESSON 1**
SUBJECT
_____ | Lesson Information/Assignment Task

Completed |

| **LESSON 2**
SUBJECT
_____ | Lesson Information/Assignment Task

Completed |

| **LESSON 3**
SUBJECT
_____ | Lesson Information/Assignment Task

Completed |

| **LESSON 4**
SUBJECT
_____ | Lesson Information/Assignment Task

Completed |

| **LESSON 5**
SUBJECT
_____ | Lesson Information/Assignment Task

Completed |

DATE / /

| **LESSON 1**
SUBJECT
_____ | Lesson Information/Assignment Task

Completed |

| **LESSON 2**
SUBJECT
_____ | Lesson Information/Assignment Task

Completed |

| **LESSON 3**
SUBJECT
_____ | Lesson Information/Assignment Task

Completed |

| **LESSON 4**
SUBJECT
_____ | Lesson Information/Assignment Task

Completed |

| **LESSON 5**
SUBJECT
_____ | Lesson Information/Assignment Task

Completed |

DATE / /

| **LESSON 1**
SUBJECT
_____ | Lesson Information/Assignment Task

Completed |

| **LESSON 2**
SUBJECT
_____ | Lesson Information/Assignment Task

Completed |

| **LESSON 3**
SUBJECT
_____ | Lesson Information/Assignment Task

Completed |

| **LESSON 4**
SUBJECT
_____ | Lesson Information/Assignment Task

Completed |

| **LESSON 5**
SUBJECT
_____ | Lesson Information/Assignment Task

Completed |

DATE / /

| **LESSON 1**
SUBJECT
_____ | Lesson Information/Assignment Task

Completed |

| **LESSON 2**
SUBJECT
_____ | Lesson Information/Assignment Task

Completed |

| **LESSON 3**
SUBJECT
_____ | Lesson Information/Assignment Task

Completed |

| **LESSON 4**
SUBJECT
_____ | Lesson Information/Assignment Task

Completed |

| **LESSON 5**
SUBJECT
_____ | Lesson Information/Assignment Task

Completed |

DATE / /

LESSON 1 SUBJECT _____	Lesson Information/Assignment Task Completed
LESSON 2 SUBJECT _____	Lesson Information/Assignment Task Completed
LESSON 3 SUBJECT _____	Lesson Information/Assignment Task Completed
LESSON 4 SUBJECT _____	Lesson Information/Assignment Task Completed
LESSON 5 SUBJECT _____	Lesson Information/Assignment Task Completed

DATE / /

LESSON 1 SUBJECT _____	Lesson Information/Assignment Task Completed
LESSON 2 SUBJECT _____	Lesson Information/Assignment Task Completed
LESSON 3 SUBJECT _____	Lesson Information/Assignment Task Completed
LESSON 4 SUBJECT _____	Lesson Information/Assignment Task Completed
LESSON 5 SUBJECT _____	Lesson Information/Assignment Task Completed

Progress Tracker

What are my current Top 5 Priorities I need to action?

1. _____

_____ Target Date to Complete ___ / ___ / ___

2. _____

_____ Target Date to Complete ___ / ___ / ___

3. _____

_____ Target Date to Complete ___ / ___ / ___

4. _____

_____ Target Date to Complete ___ / ___ / ___

5. _____

_____ Target Date to Complete ___ / ___ / ___

Other Notes or Details

DATE / /

LESSON 1 SUBJECT _____	Lesson Information/Assignment Task Completed
LESSON 2 SUBJECT _____	Lesson Information/Assignment Task Completed
LESSON 3 SUBJECT _____	Lesson Information/Assignment Task Completed
LESSON 4 SUBJECT _____	Lesson Information/Assignment Task Completed
LESSON 5 SUBJECT _____	Lesson Information/Assignment Task Completed

DATE / /

LESSON 1 SUBJECT _____	Lesson Information/Assignment Task Completed
LESSON 2 SUBJECT _____	Lesson Information/Assignment Task Completed
LESSON 3 SUBJECT _____	Lesson Information/Assignment Task Completed
LESSON 4 SUBJECT _____	Lesson Information/Assignment Task Completed
LESSON 5 SUBJECT _____	Lesson Information/Assignment Task Completed

DATE / /

LESSON 1 SUBJECT _____	Lesson Information/Assignment Task
	Completed
LESSON 2 SUBJECT _____	Lesson Information/Assignment Task
	Completed
LESSON 3 SUBJECT _____	Lesson Information/Assignment Task
	Completed
LESSON 4 SUBJECT _____	Lesson Information/Assignment Task
	Completed
LESSON 5 SUBJECT _____	Lesson Information/Assignment Task
	Completed

DATE / /

LESSON 1 SUBJECT _____	Lesson Information/Assignment Task
	Completed
LESSON 2 SUBJECT _____	Lesson Information/Assignment Task
	Completed
LESSON 3 SUBJECT _____	Lesson Information/Assignment Task
	Completed
LESSON 4 SUBJECT _____	Lesson Information/Assignment Task
	Completed
LESSON 5 SUBJECT _____	Lesson Information/Assignment Task
	Completed

DATE / /

LESSON 1
SUBJECT
_____

Lesson Information/Assignment Task

Completed

LESSON 2
SUBJECT
_____

Lesson Information/Assignment Task

Completed

LESSON 3
SUBJECT
_____

Lesson Information/Assignment Task

Completed

LESSON 4
SUBJECT
_____

Lesson Information/Assignment Task

Completed

LESSON 5
SUBJECT
_____

Lesson Information/Assignment Task

Completed

DATE / /

LESSON 1
SUBJECT
_____

Lesson Information/Assignment Task

Completed

LESSON 2
SUBJECT
_____

Lesson Information/Assignment Task

Completed

LESSON 3
SUBJECT
_____

Lesson Information/Assignment Task

Completed

LESSON 4
SUBJECT
_____

Lesson Information/Assignment Task

Completed

LESSON 5
SUBJECT
_____

Lesson Information/Assignment Task

Completed

DATE ___ / ___ / ___

LESSON 1 SUBJECT _____	Lesson Information/Assignment Task Completed
LESSON 2 SUBJECT _____	Lesson Information/Assignment Task Completed
LESSON 3 SUBJECT _____	Lesson Information/Assignment Task Completed
LESSON 4 SUBJECT _____	Lesson Information/Assignment Task Completed
LESSON 5 SUBJECT _____	Lesson Information/Assignment Task Completed

DATE ___ / ___ / ___

LESSON 1 SUBJECT _____	Lesson Information/Assignment Task Completed
LESSON 2 SUBJECT _____	Lesson Information/Assignment Task Completed
LESSON 3 SUBJECT _____	Lesson Information/Assignment Task Completed
LESSON 4 SUBJECT _____	Lesson Information/Assignment Task Completed
LESSON 5 SUBJECT _____	Lesson Information/Assignment Task Completed

DATE / /

LESSON 1 SUBJECT _____	Lesson Information/Assignment Task Completed
LESSON 2 SUBJECT _____	Lesson Information/Assignment Task Completed
LESSON 3 SUBJECT _____	Lesson Information/Assignment Task Completed
LESSON 4 SUBJECT _____	Lesson Information/Assignment Task Completed
LESSON 5 SUBJECT _____	Lesson Information/Assignment Task Completed

DATE / /

LESSON 1 SUBJECT _____	Lesson Information/Assignment Task Completed
LESSON 2 SUBJECT _____	Lesson Information/Assignment Task Completed
LESSON 3 SUBJECT _____	Lesson Information/Assignment Task Completed
LESSON 4 SUBJECT _____	Lesson Information/Assignment Task Completed
LESSON 5 SUBJECT _____	Lesson Information/Assignment Task Completed

DATE / /

LESSON 1
SUBJECT

Lesson Information/Assignment Task

Completed

LESSON 2
SUBJECT

Lesson Information/Assignment Task

Completed

LESSON 3
SUBJECT

Lesson Information/Assignment Task

Completed

LESSON 4
SUBJECT

Lesson Information/Assignment Task

Completed

LESSON 5
SUBJECT

Lesson Information/Assignment Task

Completed

DATE / /

LESSON 1
SUBJECT

Lesson Information/Assignment Task

Completed

LESSON 2
SUBJECT

Lesson Information/Assignment Task

Completed

LESSON 3
SUBJECT

Lesson Information/Assignment Task

Completed

LESSON 4
SUBJECT

Lesson Information/Assignment Task

Completed

LESSON 5
SUBJECT

Lesson Information/Assignment Task

Completed

DATE / /

LESSON 1
SUBJECT

_____

Lesson Information/Assignment Task

Completed

LESSON 2
SUBJECT

_____

Lesson Information/Assignment Task

Completed

LESSON 3
SUBJECT

_____

Lesson Information/Assignment Task

Completed

LESSON 4
SUBJECT

_____

Lesson Information/Assignment Task

Completed

LESSON 5
SUBJECT

_____

Lesson Information/Assignment Task

Completed

DATE / /

LESSON 1
SUBJECT

_____

Lesson Information/Assignment Task

Completed

LESSON 2
SUBJECT

_____

Lesson Information/Assignment Task

Completed

LESSON 3
SUBJECT

_____

Lesson Information/Assignment Task

Completed

LESSON 4
SUBJECT

_____

Lesson Information/Assignment Task

Completed

LESSON 5
SUBJECT

_____

Lesson Information/Assignment Task

Completed

DATE ___/___/___

LESSON 1
SUBJECT
_____

Lesson Information/Assignment Task

Completed

LESSON 2
SUBJECT
_____

Lesson Information/Assignment Task

Completed

LESSON 3
SUBJECT
_____

Lesson Information/Assignment Task

Completed

LESSON 4
SUBJECT
_____

Lesson Information/Assignment Task

Completed

LESSON 5
SUBJECT
_____

Lesson Information/Assignment Task

Completed

DATE ___/___/___

LESSON 1
SUBJECT
_____

Lesson Information/Assignment Task

Completed

LESSON 2
SUBJECT
_____

Lesson Information/Assignment Task

Completed

LESSON 3
SUBJECT
_____

Lesson Information/Assignment Task

Completed

LESSON 4
SUBJECT
_____

Lesson Information/Assignment Task

Completed

LESSON 5
SUBJECT
_____

Lesson Information/Assignment Task

Completed

DATE   /   /

LESSON 1 SUBJECT _____	Lesson Information/Assignment Task
	Completed
LESSON 2 SUBJECT _____	Lesson Information/Assignment Task
	Completed
LESSON 3 SUBJECT _____	Lesson Information/Assignment Task
	Completed
LESSON 4 SUBJECT _____	Lesson Information/Assignment Task
	Completed
LESSON 5 SUBJECT _____	Lesson Information/Assignment Task
	Completed

DATE   /   /

LESSON 1 SUBJECT _____	Lesson Information/Assignment Task
	Completed
LESSON 2 SUBJECT _____	Lesson Information/Assignment Task
	Completed
LESSON 3 SUBJECT _____	Lesson Information/Assignment Task
	Completed
LESSON 4 SUBJECT _____	Lesson Information/Assignment Task
	Completed
LESSON 5 SUBJECT _____	Lesson Information/Assignment Task
	Completed

DATE   /   /

LESSON 1
SUBJECT

_____

Lesson Information/Assignment Task

Completed

LESSON 2
SUBJECT

_____

Lesson Information/Assignment Task

Completed

LESSON 3
SUBJECT

_____

Lesson Information/Assignment Task

Completed

LESSON 4
SUBJECT

_____

Lesson Information/Assignment Task

Completed

LESSON 5
SUBJECT

_____

Lesson Information/Assignment Task

Completed

DATE   /   /

LESSON 1
SUBJECT

_____

Lesson Information/Assignment Task

Completed

LESSON 2
SUBJECT

_____

Lesson Information/Assignment Task

Completed

LESSON 3
SUBJECT

_____

Lesson Information/Assignment Task

Completed

LESSON 4
SUBJECT

_____

Lesson Information/Assignment Task

Completed

LESSON 5
SUBJECT

_____

Lesson Information/Assignment Task

Completed

DATE   /   /

LESSON 1 SUBJECT _____	Lesson Information/Assignment Task
	Completed
LESSON 2 SUBJECT _____	Lesson Information/Assignment Task
	Completed
LESSON 3 SUBJECT _____	Lesson Information/Assignment Task
	Completed
LESSON 4 SUBJECT _____	Lesson Information/Assignment Task
	Completed
LESSON 5 SUBJECT _____	Lesson Information/Assignment Task
	Completed

DATE   /   /

LESSON 1 SUBJECT _____	Lesson Information/Assignment Task
	Completed
LESSON 2 SUBJECT _____	Lesson Information/Assignment Task
	Completed
LESSON 3 SUBJECT _____	Lesson Information/Assignment Task
	Completed
LESSON 4 SUBJECT _____	Lesson Information/Assignment Task
	Completed
LESSON 5 SUBJECT _____	Lesson Information/Assignment Task
	Completed

DATE / /

LESSON 1 SUBJECT _____	Lesson Information/Assignment Task Completed
LESSON 2 SUBJECT _____	Lesson Information/Assignment Task Completed
LESSON 3 SUBJECT _____	Lesson Information/Assignment Task Completed
LESSON 4 SUBJECT _____	Lesson Information/Assignment Task Completed
LESSON 5 SUBJECT _____	Lesson Information/Assignment Task Completed

DATE / /

LESSON 1 SUBJECT _____	Lesson Information/Assignment Task Completed
LESSON 2 SUBJECT _____	Lesson Information/Assignment Task Completed
LESSON 3 SUBJECT _____	Lesson Information/Assignment Task Completed
LESSON 4 SUBJECT _____	Lesson Information/Assignment Task Completed
LESSON 5 SUBJECT _____	Lesson Information/Assignment Task Completed

DATE / /

LESSON 1 SUBJECT _____	Lesson Information/Assignment Task Completed
LESSON 2 SUBJECT _____	Lesson Information/Assignment Task Completed
LESSON 3 SUBJECT _____	Lesson Information/Assignment Task Completed
LESSON 4 SUBJECT _____	Lesson Information/Assignment Task Completed
LESSON 5 SUBJECT _____	Lesson Information/Assignment Task Completed

DATE / /

LESSON 1 SUBJECT _____	Lesson Information/Assignment Task Completed
LESSON 2 SUBJECT _____	Lesson Information/Assignment Task Completed
LESSON 3 SUBJECT _____	Lesson Information/Assignment Task Completed
LESSON 4 SUBJECT _____	Lesson Information/Assignment Task Completed
LESSON 5 SUBJECT _____	Lesson Information/Assignment Task Completed

DATE / /

LESSON 1 SUBJECT _____	Lesson Information/Assignment Task
	Completed
LESSON 2 SUBJECT _____	Lesson Information/Assignment Task
	Completed
LESSON 3 SUBJECT _____	Lesson Information/Assignment Task
	Completed
LESSON 4 SUBJECT _____	Lesson Information/Assignment Task
	Completed
LESSON 5 SUBJECT _____	Lesson Information/Assignment Task
	Completed

DATE / /

LESSON 1 SUBJECT _____	Lesson Information/Assignment Task
	Completed
LESSON 2 SUBJECT _____	Lesson Information/Assignment Task
	Completed
LESSON 3 SUBJECT _____	Lesson Information/Assignment Task
	Completed
LESSON 4 SUBJECT _____	Lesson Information/Assignment Task
	Completed
LESSON 5 SUBJECT _____	Lesson Information/Assignment Task
	Completed

DATE / /

LESSON 1
SUBJECT

_____

Lesson Information/Assignment Task

Completed

LESSON 2
SUBJECT

_____

Lesson Information/Assignment Task

Completed

LESSON 3
SUBJECT

_____

Lesson Information/Assignment Task

Completed

LESSON 4
SUBJECT

_____

Lesson Information/Assignment Task

Completed

LESSON 5
SUBJECT

_____

Lesson Information/Assignment Task

Completed

DATE / /

LESSON 1
SUBJECT

_____

Lesson Information/Assignment Task

Completed

LESSON 2
SUBJECT

_____

Lesson Information/Assignment Task

Completed

LESSON 3
SUBJECT

_____

Lesson Information/Assignment Task

Completed

LESSON 4
SUBJECT

_____

Lesson Information/Assignment Task

Completed

LESSON 5
SUBJECT

_____

Lesson Information/Assignment Task

Completed

DATE / /

LESSON 1 SUBJECT _____	Lesson Information/Assignment Task
	Completed

LESSON 2 SUBJECT _____	Lesson Information/Assignment Task
	Completed

LESSON 3 SUBJECT _____	Lesson Information/Assignment Task
	Completed

LESSON 4 SUBJECT _____	Lesson Information/Assignment Task
	Completed

LESSON 5 SUBJECT _____	Lesson Information/Assignment Task
	Completed

DATE / /

LESSON 1 SUBJECT _____	Lesson Information/Assignment Task
	Completed

LESSON 2 SUBJECT _____	Lesson Information/Assignment Task
	Completed

LESSON 3 SUBJECT _____	Lesson Information/Assignment Task
	Completed

LESSON 4 SUBJECT _____	Lesson Information/Assignment Task
	Completed

LESSON 5 SUBJECT _____	Lesson Information/Assignment Task
	Completed

notes. _____

The
HOMESCHOOL
Teacher's
Lesson Planner and Organizer

MAJOR ASSIGNMENTS

MAJOR ASSIGNMENTS

DATE:

Subject:	Assignment/task

Notes

Grade

Signature _____ Date _____

DATE:

Subject:	Assignment/task

Notes

Grade

Signature _____ Date _____

MAJOR ASSIGNMENTS

DATE:

Subject:	Assignment/task

Notes

Grade

Signature _____ Date _____

DATE:

Subject:	Assignment/task

Notes

Grade

Signature _____ Date _____

MAJOR ASSIGNMENTS

DATE:

Subject:	Assignment/task

Notes

Grade

Signature _____ Date _____

DATE:

Subject:	Assignment/task

Notes

Grade

Signature _____ Date _____

MAJOR ASSIGNMENTS

DATE:

Subject:	Assignment/task

Notes

Grade

Signature _____ Date _____

DATE:

Subject:	Assignment/task

Notes

Grade

Signature _____ Date _____

MAJOR ASSIGNMENTS

DATE:

Subject:	Assignment/task

Notes

Grade

Signature _____ Date _____

DATE:

Subject:	Assignment/task

Notes

Grade

Signature _____ Date _____

MAJOR ASSIGNMENTS

DATE:

Subject:	Assignment/task

Notes

Grade

Signature _____ Date _____

DATE:

Subject:	Assignment/task

Notes

Grade

Signature _____ Date _____

MAJOR ASSIGNMENTS

DATE:

Subject:	Assignment/task

Notes

Grade

Signature _____ Date _____

DATE:

Subject:	Assignment/task

Notes

Grade

Signature _____ Date _____

MAJOR ASSIGNMENTS

DATE:

Subject:	Assignment/task

Notes

Grade

Signature _____ **Date** _____

DATE:

Subject:	Assignment/task

Notes

Grade

Signature _____ **Date** _____

MAJOR ASSIGNMENTS

DATE:

Subject:	Assignment/task

Notes

Grade

Signature _____ Date _____

DATE:

Subject:	Assignment/task

Notes

Grade

Signature _____ Date _____

MAJOR ASSIGNMENTS

DATE:

Subject:	Assignment/task

Notes

Grade

Signature _____ Date _____

DATE:

Subject:	Assignment/task

Notes

Grade

Signature _____ Date _____

MAJOR ASSIGNMENTS

DATE:

Subject:	Assignment/task

Notes

Grade

Signature _____ **Date** _____

DATE:

Subject:	Assignment/task

Notes

Grade

Signature _____ **Date** _____

MAJOR ASSIGNMENTS

DATE:

Subject:	Assignment/task

Notes

Grade

Signature _____ Date _____

DATE:

Subject:	Assignment/task

Notes

Grade

Signature _____ Date _____

notes.

The
HOMESCHOOL
Teacher's
Lesson Planner and Organizer

REPORT CARDS

report card._____

DATE [   ] **SCHOOL YEAR LEVEL** [   ]

STUDENT NAME [   ]

AGE [   ] **REPORTING PERIOD** EG. Sept – Nov [   ]

....

SUBJECT [   ] **GRADE** [   ]

COMMENTS

[   ]

SUBJECT [   ] **GRADE** [   ]

COMMENTS

[   ]

SUBJECT [   ] **GRADE** [   ]

COMMENTS

[   ]

report card. _____

SUBJECT [   ] **GRADE** [   ]

COMMENTS

[   ]

SUBJECT [   ] **GRADE** [   ]

COMMENTS

[   ]

SUBJECT [   ] **GRADE** [   ]

COMMENTS

[   ]

SUBJECT [   ] **GRADE** [   ]

COMMENTS

[   ]

report card. _____

DATE [　　　　　　　] **SCHOOL YEAR LEVEL** [　　　]

STUDENT NAME [　　　　　　　　　　　　　　　　]

AGE [　　　] **REPORTING PERIOD** EG. Sept – Nov [　　　　　　]

....

SUBJECT [　　　　　　　　　　　　　　] **GRADE** [　　]

COMMENTS

[　　　　　　　　　　　　　　　　　　　　　　　　　]

SUBJECT [　　　　　　　　　　　　　　] **GRADE** [　　]

COMMENTS

[　　　　　　　　　　　　　　　　　　　　　　　　　]

SUBJECT [　　　　　　　　　　　　　　] **GRADE** [　　]

COMMENTS

[　　　　　　　　　　　　　　　　　　　　　　　　　]

report card.

SUBJECT [   ]   **GRADE** [   ]

COMMENTS

[   ]

SUBJECT [   ]   **GRADE** [   ]

COMMENTS

[   ]

SUBJECT [   ]   **GRADE** [   ]

COMMENTS

[   ]

SUBJECT [   ]   **GRADE** [   ]

COMMENTS

[   ]

report card._____

DATE [_____]   **SCHOOL YEAR LEVEL** [_____]

STUDENT NAME [_____]

AGE [_____]   **REPORTING PERIOD** EG. Sept – Nov [_____]

....

SUBJECT [_____]   **GRADE** [_____]

COMMENTS

[_____]

SUBJECT [_____]   **GRADE** [_____]

COMMENTS

[_____]

SUBJECT [_____]   **GRADE** [_____]

COMMENTS

[_____]

report card._____

SUBJECT [   ]   **GRADE** [   ]

COMMENTS

[   ]

SUBJECT [   ]   **GRADE** [   ]

COMMENTS

[   ]

SUBJECT [   ]   **GRADE** [   ]

COMMENTS

[   ]

SUBJECT [   ]   **GRADE** [   ]

COMMENTS

[   ]

report card. _____

DATE [　　　　　] **SCHOOL YEAR LEVEL** [　　]

STUDENT NAME [　　　　　　　　　　　　　　　　　　]

AGE [　　] **REPORTING PERIOD** EG. Sept – Nov [　　　　　]

....

SUBJECT [　　　　　　　　　　　　　　] **GRADE** [　　]

COMMENTS

[　　　　　　　　　　　　　　　　　　　　　　　　　　]

SUBJECT [　　　　　　　　　　　　　　] **GRADE** [　　]

COMMENTS

[　　　　　　　　　　　　　　　　　　　　　　　　　　]

SUBJECT [　　　　　　　　　　　　　　] **GRADE** [　　]

COMMENTS

[　　　　　　　　　　　　　　　　　　　　　　　　　　]

report card. _____

SUBJECT [   ] **GRADE** [   ]

COMMENTS

[   ]

SUBJECT [   ] **GRADE** [   ]

COMMENTS

[   ]

SUBJECT [   ] **GRADE** [   ]

COMMENTS

[   ]

SUBJECT [   ] **GRADE** [   ]

COMMENTS

[   ]

notes. _____

notes.

notes.

notes.

ORDER YOUR NEXT COPY OF THE

The
HOMESCHOOL
Teacher's
Planner

TODAY!

and be organized for your next school year.

Available on all major online bookstores OR VISIT www.thelifegraduate.com to order your new copy.

THE HOMESCHOOL
STUDENT PLANNER 🏠

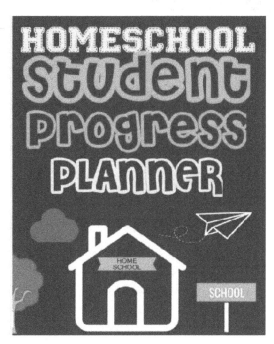

Purchase yours today via any major online
bookstore or via

www.thelifegraduate.com

The Homeschool
Student Progress Planner includes:
- A template for students to include their Weekly Timetable
- Weekly Planning to include all Class Lessons and Subjects
- A weekly gratitude log
- Self-Reporting Attendance Log
- Templates to Record Subject and Assignment Tasks
- Templates for the Homeschool Teacher/Parent to complete subject reports
- 8.5 x 11 inch to provide ample room to provide information
- 140 pages
- Makes an excellent companion to The Homeschool Teacher Planner resource

The
HOMESCHOOL
Teacher's
Lesson Planner and Organizer

CPSIA information can be obtained
at www.ICGtesting.com
Printed in the USA
LVHW051103050821
694613LV00007B/300